ROCK-OLOGY
The Hard Facts
About Rocks

Baking and Crushing
A Look at Metamorphic Rock

by Ellen Lawrence

Consultants:

Shawn W. Wallace
Department of Earth and Planetary Sciences
American Museum of Natural History, New York, New York

Kimberly Brenneman, PhD
National Institute for Early Education Research, Rutgers University
New Brunswick, New Jersey

BEARPORT
PUBLISHING

New York, New York

Credits

Cover, © MIXA/Alamy; 2–3T, © vvoe/Shutterstock; 2–3M, © Siim Sepp/Shutterstock; 2–3B, © Siim Sepp/Shutterstock; 4–5, © Tupungato/Shutterstock; 6, © Siim Sepp/Shutterstock; 7, © MIXA/Alamy; 8T, © OlegSam/Shutterstock; 8B, © Siim Sepp/Shutterstock; 9L, © Colin D. Young/Shutterstock; 9C, © David Salcedo/Shutterstock; 9R, © Shutterstock; 10–11, © Shutterstock; 12T, © Dr Ajay Kumar Singh/Shutterstock; 12B, © vvoe/Shutterstock; 13, © Shutterstock; 14B, © Wanchai Orsuk/Shutterstock; 14–15, © Dr Juerg Alean/Science Photo Library; 16–17, © LianeM/Alamy; 18, © PF-(usna)/Alamy; 19, © Ververidis Vasilis/Shutterstock; 19R, © Markus Gann/Shutterstock, © B art/Shutterstock, © Wiratchai wansamngam/Shutterstock, and © Destinyweddingstudio/Shutterstock; 20, © Ziviani/Shutterstock; 21, © Siim Sepp/Shutterstock, © Tom Grundy/Shutterstock, © marekuliasz/Shutterstock, © Zadiraka Evgenii/Shutterstock, and © Tyler Boyes/Shutterstock; 22T, © GOLFX/Shutterstock; 22M (2 images), © Ruby Tuesday Books; 22B, © Maria Bobrova/Shutterstock; 23TL, © Myszka/Shutterstock; 23TC, © Christopher Ewing/Shutterstock; 23TR, © Martin Fowler/Shutterstock; 23BL, © Ververidis Vasilis/Shutterstock; 23BC, © Bork/Shutterstock; 23BR, © JeniFoto/Shutterstock.

Publisher: Kenn Goin
Editorial Director: Adam Siegel
Creative Director: Spencer Brinker
Project Editor: Natalie Lunis
Photo Researcher: Ruby Tuesday Books Ltd

Library of Congress Cataloging-in-Publication Data

Lawrence, Ellen, 1967– author.
  Baking and crushing : a look at metamorphic rock / by Ellen Lawrence.
      pages cm. — (Rock-ology)
  Audience: Ages 7–12.
  Includes bibliographical references and index.
  ISBN 978-1-62724-300-1 (library binding) — ISBN 1-62724-300-3 (library binding)
  1. Metamorphic rocks—Juvenile literature. 2. Metamorphism (Geology)—Juvenile literature. I. Title.
  QE475.A2L39 2015
  552.4—dc23
                                        2014014016

For more information, write to Bearport Publishing Company, Inc., 45 West 21st Street, Suite 3B, New York, New York 10010. Printed in the United States of America.

10 9 8 7 6 5 4 3 2 1

Contents

A Statue Made from Rock 4

Metamorphic Rock 6

Changing Rock......................... 8

Inside Earth's Crust 10

Baking New Rock 12

Crushing and Baking.................... 14

Finding Marble 16

Marble for a Statue 18

Check Out Some Rocks 20

Science Lab........................... 22

Science Words 23

Index................................. 24

Read More............................ 24

Learn More Online...................... 24

About the Author....................... 24

A Statue Made from Rock

In Washington, D.C., there is a huge statue of President Abraham Lincoln.

The beautiful statue is shiny, white, and smooth.

It's hard to believe that it's made of rock—but it is!

The statue is made from a kind of rock called marble.

Where does marble come from, and how does this rock form?

The statue of Abraham Lincoln was carved from marble by artists called **sculptors**. It is 19 feet (5.8 m) tall from Lincoln's shoes to the top of his head.

marble

Metamorphic Rock

Marble is a type of rock called **metamorphic** rock.

The name *metamorphic* comes from a Greek word that means "change in form."

A metamorphic rock is a rock that has changed.

It started out as one kind of rock and then changed into a different kind!

marble

soapstone

There are many other metamorphic rocks besides marble. Soapstone and hornfels are some other metamorphic rocks.

cliffs made of hornfels

Changing Rock

Scientists sort rocks into three main types called metamorphic, **sedimentary,** and **igneous** rocks.

Sometimes igneous rocks change into metamorphic rocks.

Sedimentary rocks can change into metamorphic rocks, too.

Marble forms from a kind of sedimentary rock called limestone.

Where does this amazing change take place?

granite (igneous rock)

changes into

gneiss (metamorphic rock)

Gneiss (NICE) is another kind of metamorphic rock. Gneiss can form from an igneous rock called granite.

metamorphic rock

sedimentary rock

igneous rock

What do you think might happen to a rock to make it change from one kind to another?

Inside Earth's Crust

Marble forms from limestone inside Earth's crust.

The crust is the rocky outer layer of Earth.

Beneath the crust, there is super-hot melted rock called **magma**.

Heat from magma can change rocks from one kind to another.

How does this happen?

Earth's crust is made up of many different kinds of rock, including granite, slate, sandstone, and limestone. In its thickest places, the rocky crust is more than 50 miles (80 km) deep.

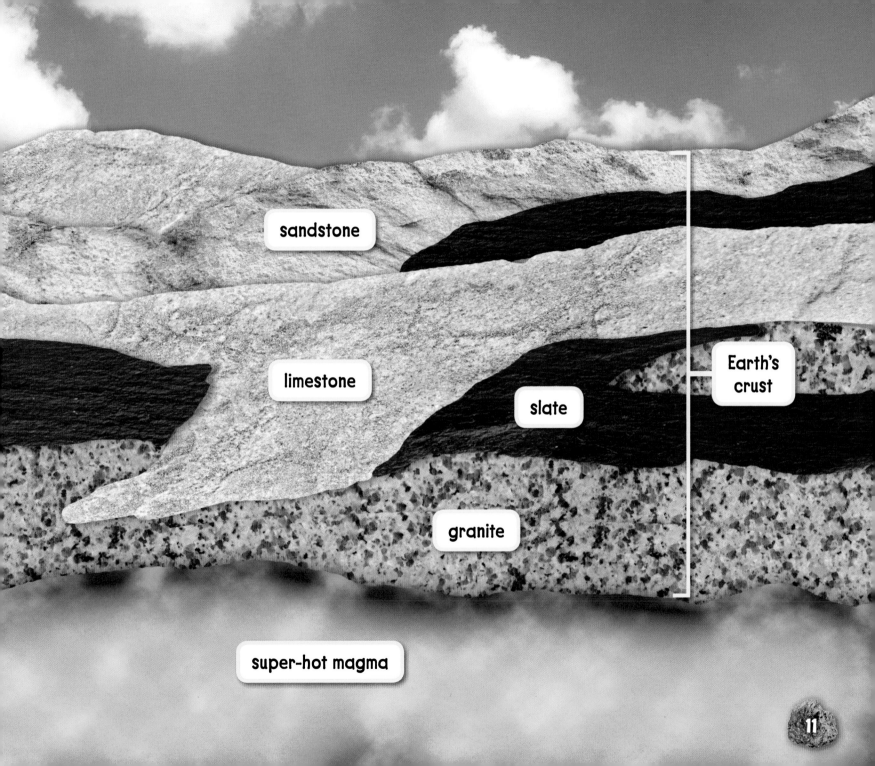

sandstone

limestone

slate

Earth's crust

granite

super-hot magma

Baking New Rock

Sometimes a crack forms deep in Earth's crust.

Then super-hot magma oozes into the crack.

The extreme heat from the magma bakes the rock around the crack.

When limestone gets baked in this way, it starts to change.

It can take thousands of years, but eventually the limestone changes into marble!

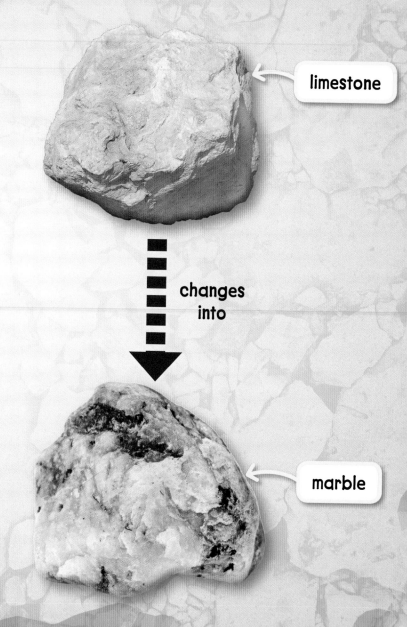

limestone

changes into

marble

12

crack in Earth's crust

limestone that has changed into marble

limestone

heat from magma

heat from magma

Limestone is not the only kind of rock that can be baked and changed into metamorphic rock. Heat from magma can change any kind of rock into metamorphic rock by baking it.

super-hot magma

Crushing and Baking

It's not only heat from magma that can form metamorphic rock.

Sometimes, when Earth's crust cracks, it causes huge movements.

As the crust moves, rocks are crushed, stretched, folded, and rubbed against each other.

These movements produce lots of heat, which bakes the rocks.

Being crushed and baked can make rocks change into new kinds of rocks.

When rocks are crushed and rubbed together, heat is produced. You can feel how this happens by pushing the palms of your hands together and rubbing hard. Try it and describe what you feel.

It's sometimes possible to see the folds in metamorphic rocks. For example, this gneiss has a swirled pattern that shows how it was folded and stretched as it formed.

folds in gneiss

Finding Marble

Marble and other kinds of metamorphic rock form deep underground in Earth's crust.

So how is it possible for people to find and use these rocks?

Sometimes wind and rain wear away rock on Earth's surface.

The top layers of rock crumble and break up.

Then they are washed or blown away.

Slowly, over millions of years, rock that was once underground becomes Earth's outer layer.

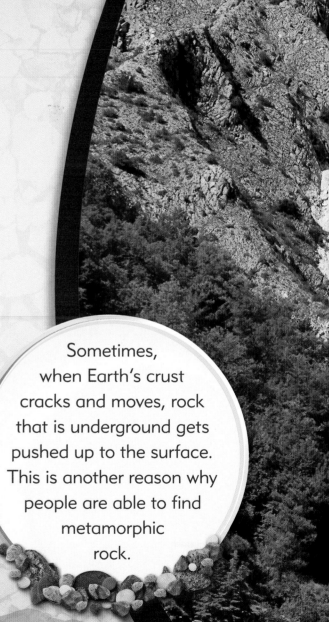

Sometimes, when Earth's crust cracks and moves, rock that is underground gets pushed up to the surface. This is another reason why people are able to find metamorphic rock.

17

Marble for a Statue

People get marble and other rock from places called **quarries**.

Quarry workers cut giant blocks of marble from mountainsides or from the ground.

The marble used to make Lincoln's statue was cut from a quarry about 100 years ago.

The marble formed deep underground, however, about 500 million years ago!

workers constructing Lincoln's statue

The marble statue of President Lincoln was carved from 28 blocks of marble. The marble came from a quarry in Georgia.

marble quarry

When marble forms, it doesn't always look the same. Look at these pictures. In what ways are the different types of marble alike? How are they different?

19

Check Out Some Rocks

Baking and crushing changes sedimentary and igneous rocks into metamorphic rocks.

So what happens to metamorphic rocks if they are baked and crushed?

When this happens, metamorphic rocks change, too.

They change into new kinds of metamorphic rocks!

At this moment, rocks are changing into new rocks inside Earth's crust—deep beneath your feet!

Metamorphic Rock Chart

This chart shows some metamorphic rocks.

It also shows the kinds of rocks they were before they were changed.

sandstone
(sedimentary)

quartzite
(metamorphic)

shale
(sedimentary)

slate
(metamorphic)

gabbro
(igneous)

amphibolite
(metamorphic)

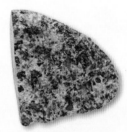

basalt
(igneous)

schist
(metamorphic)

slate
(metamorphic)

phyllite
(metamorphic)

Science Lab

Make Metamorphic Rock

Using modeling clay, you can show how metamorphic rocks form from other rocks.

1. Use different colored clay to make a model of sedimentary rock. This type of rock often has rocky layers that are different colors.

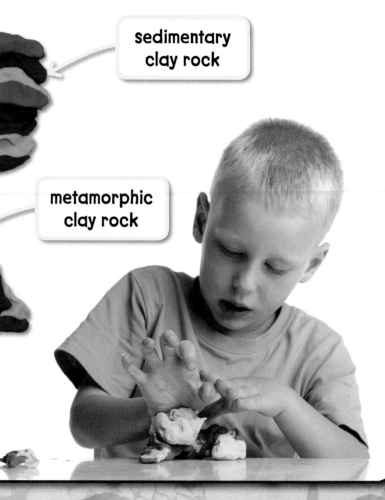

sedimentary clay rock

2. Squeeze, fold, and stretch your clay rock in your hands to turn it into metamorphic rock.

metamorphic clay rock

Your piece of clay rock still has the same ingredients. By crushing it, though, you've changed it into a new kind of rock!

Science Words

igneous (IG-nee-uhss) one of the three main types of rock; basalt, gabbro, and granite are kinds of igneous rock

magma (MAG-muh) super-hot liquid rock found deep inside Earth

metamorphic (*met*-uh-MOR-fik) one of the three main types of rock; marble, slate, and gneiss are kinds of metamorphic rock

quarries (KWOR-eez) places in the ground or along the sides of hills where rock, such as marble or granite, is cut

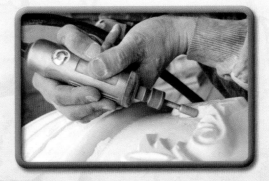

sculptors (SKUHLP-turz) artists who use tools to carve statues and other objects from rock

sedimentary (*sed*-uh-MEN-tuh-ree) one of the three main types of rock; sandstone, limestone, and shale are kinds of sedimentary rock

Index

baking 12–13, 14, 20

crushing 14, 20, 22

crust 10–11, 12–13, 14, 16, 20

Earth 10–11, 12, 14, 16, 20

gneiss 8, 15

granite 8, 10–11

hornfels 6–7

igneous rock 8, 20

limestone 8–9, 10–11, 12–13

Lincoln, Abraham 4–5, 18

magma 10–11, 12–13

marble 4–5, 6, 8–9, 10, 12–13, 16–17, 18–19

metamorphic rock 6, 8, 13, 14–15, 16, 20–21, 22

quarries 18–19

sandstone 10–11, 21

sculptors 5

sedimentary rock 8, 20, 22

slate 10–11, 21

soapstone 6

statues 4–5, 17, 18

Washington, D.C. 4

Read More

Faulkner, Rebecca. *Metamorphic Rock (Geology Rocks!).* Chicago: Raintree (2008).

Owen, Ruth. *Science and Craft Projects with Rocks and Soil (Get Crafty Outdoors).* New York: PowerKids Press (2013).

Rosinsky, Natalie M. *Rocks: Hard, Soft, Smooth, and Rough.* Minneapolis, MN: Picture Window Books (2003).

Learn More Online

To learn more about metamorphic rock, visit
www.bearportpublishing.com/Rock-ology

About the Author

Ellen Lawrence lives in the United Kingdom. Her favorite books to write are those about nature and animals. In fact, the first book Ellen bought for herself, when she was six years old, was the story of a gorilla named Patty Cake that was born in New York's Central Park Zoo.